WORKBOOK

FOR

STILLNESS IS THE KEY

BY RYAN HOLIDAY

Growth Hack Books

TABLE OF CONTENTS

PART I: MIND

CHAPTER 1: THE DOMAIN OF THE MIND

President John F. Kennedy woke one morning, in the middle of October in 1962, to news from the CIA. Soviets were closing in on the ability to strike the United States and surrounding territories with nuclear missiles from a base in Cuba. The *Cold* War was finally reaching its boiling point.

Kennedy was having a tough time in his new presidency, especially due to the inheritance of the Cold War tensions. The Bay of Pigs invasion of Cuba had failed and his political meetings with Premier Krushchev did not make him look good. Khrushchev assured Kennedy that the missiles in Cuba were merely a defensive tactic that would never be used in an act of aggression. Could Kennedy chance believing him? Millions of American lives could be lost if he made an error but he also didn't want to escalate conflict.

The CIA urged quick aggression; they wanted the missile base destroyed and followed up by a full-scale invasion of Cuba. Kennedy had been bullied by the CIA's advice over the first few months of his presidency but he started to push back. He had been reading some world history and knew how fast-acting leaders started wars which they could not contain once started. He called for a smarter strategy. Kennedy urged for patience and to understand the variables at play. He wanted to understand *why* the Russians would do this before acting. Years earlier, he wrote a review of a book on nuclear warfare and quotes a passage about allowing the enemy to exit the situation without looking bad. Giving your opponent the option to 'save face' can often end a situation without escalation and this attitude was likely weighing on Kennedy's mind during that time.

Kennedy embodied an attitude of open stillness during this time. He didn't let his ego get in the way of what was the right thing to do. He communicated with old rivals in a calm tone, let others speak, and left the room when he felt there was too much tension for clear thinking. Out of this, he came to the conclusion that there would be a blockade of Cuba until they backed down. He faced criticism from those who urged a more aggressive approach. He also faced arguments from those who suggested that the United States should do nothing. After all, they had plenty of nuclear missiles of their own pointed at the Soviets. Kennedy was sympathetic to this point of view but argued that the Soviet posturing was an act of hostility which must be met early as to avoid the mistakes of the 1930s. A looming threat must be checked.

Kennedy had plenty of stress during this time but he didn't let the stress rush him into action or freeze into inaction. He found moments of solitude to deal with his personal stress and did whatever he could to facilitate fruitful social interactions. Once the decision of the blockade was made, he had to maintain this poise to carry out the plan. Tensions would rise as he readied the 500 miles of blockade around Cuba. A Cuban submarine took to the surface and one US pilot was shot down.

But Kennedy persisted and eventually Krushchev wrote him a letter which would eventually lead to a surrendering of his position in Cuba in exchange for Kennedy promising not to invade Cuba. The crisis was averted and Kennedy saved the world from nuclear extinction through his ability to slow things down, think, but still act when needed.

In making important decisions, there are several lessons one can take from this. We must resist distractions, take our time, bring our full selves to the situation, balance our convictions against new advice, and conduct analysis without leading to paralysis. If we develop a stillness of balanced convictions, we can be like a rock which the roaring seas wash over until they calm into a state of tranquility. This stillness isn't easy to achieve but it is doable.

KNOWLEDGE RETENTION TEST

1. President Kennedy had to deal with the possibility of the Cold War.

   True [ ]

   False [ ]

2. The Bay of Pigs was in Puerto Rico.

   True [ ]

   False [ ]

3. Nobody wanted Kennedy to act aggressively.

   True [ ]

   False [ ]

4. The CIA was pushing for Kennedy to strike against Russia.

   True [ ]

   False [ ]

5. Kennedy's ability to slow down and think helped ease tensions between the two countries.

   True [ ]

   False [ ]

PREP WORK Q & A

1. What influenced Kennedy to slow down?

_____

_____

_____

_____

_____

2. Do you feel as though his approach saved lives?

_____

_____

_____

_____

_____

3. Why should you learn to control stress?

_____

_____

_____

_____

CHECKLIST

___Recall a time you made a choice while stressed.

___Think about how your reaction affected the outcome.

___Consider how you could have reacted differently.

___Understand how stress influenced the situation.

CHAPTER 2: BECOME PRESENT

Let's look at another act of presence and stillness, one that's more extreme in its needs for physical control of one's self: Marina Abramovic's appropriately titled performance *The Artist is Present.* The performance would represent her decades of learning. She was literally present at the Museum of Modern Art (MoMA) where she sat still from March 14th to May 31st 2010. That's just over 736 hours (79 days) sitting in silence.

Most of us have trouble sitting still for thirty minutes, never mind 736 hours and 30 minutes. She sat in a wooden chair and looked up at the person across from her as they replaced themselves as the hours and the days went on. She would later comment that the point is to empty yourself and just be completely present in the moment. There might be a few who question whether sitting is anything special, equating it doing nothing or being lazy. Those who visited Marina during her exhibition and sat in the chair across from her would never think that way. For them, it was a spiritual experience. They waited in line, often for hours, for a chance to sit across from her. Many patrons were often brought to tears by her ability to focus on their moment and reject the power of other stimuli.

She had to fight off hunger, daydreaming, sleepiness, discomfort, and more so the other person would sense that she is present. If she slowed down her bodily functions too much, she would fall asleep. Marina had to remain alert and yet reject a range of stimuli. This requires the strength of a warrior and the patience of a Buddhist monk. She had to constantly make sure that the task at hand, focusing on the person across from her, was the most important thing in the world. So, being present is not nothing as some might be quick to assume. It's everything. It demands from us all that we are.

There are lessons to take from this. When we are about to give a speech, we become obsessed with what others might think of us instead of thinking about the actual speech itself. We might struggle to take a picture of a sunset, or ignore it all together, instead of taking it in. We obsess about the future needs for improvement that we can't take care of the present. Even while waiting in line to see Marina, her guests skipped many of her other works of art to see her current performance. They twitched, checked out phones, paced nervously, and checked their phones again. Hopefully, they learned something from their brief encounter with Marina but it is more likely that most returned to being slaves to a swaying attention that makes presence and true focus impossible.

Your current moment, obstacle, decision, relationship, or object of your attention requires your full being. None of us are so talented that we can bring half of ourselves to the present moment and expect to live fully. You must not waste your energy by living in the past or future when the present requires all of that energy. We must moderate our inputs to be able to do this.

KNOWLEDGE RETENTION TEST

1. Marina Abramovic sat still for over 700 hours for her art.

   True [ ]

   False [ ]

2. No one came and visited her.

   True [ ]

   False [ ]

3. Staying present can be a challenge.

   True [ ]

   False [ ]

4. People struggle to actually stay in the present moment without doing anything else.

   True [ ]

   False [ ]

5. Living in the past or future takes away from the present.

   True [ ]

   False [ ]

PREP WORK Q & A

1. How do people avoid being in the present?

   _____

   _____

   _____

   _____

   _____

2. What did Marina Abramovic have to deal with to stay present?

   _____

   _____

   _____

   _____

   _____

3. What requires your full being?

   _____

   _____

   _____

   _____

   _____

CHECKLIST

____Understand what being present means.

____Pay attention to how you avoid being present.

____Practice allowing yourself to be present.

____Give yourself time to learn to be present.

CHAPTER 3: LIMIT YOUR INPUTS

Napoleon was certainly an odd leader and a bit unconventional in his approach. He was, however, rather selective with how his focus was divided. He would have his secretary wait three weeks before opening any new mail. He enjoyed finding out how many issues were resolved on their own without any need to waste his attention on the mail he received. He was much more attentive to his soldiers but prioritized bad news. In fact, he told them to never wake him up with any good news. It didn't matter how significant the gain was, he only needed to know the bad news. He specified to wake him up instantly with bad news so he can address it immediately.

We all need a system that helps us filter out useless information. A general analytical personality and proclivity towards deep thought are not enough. A true leader, a truly successful person, must carve out time and a corresponding space specifically to think through important issues. You can't rely on the flow of your attention which will often lead you astray and betray you at almost every turn.

This has become increasingly difficult in the modern age. 24-hour news networks and a constant stream of data keeps us reactionary. We try to stay 'on top' of things and stay evolving but we really never grow because we don't take the time to extract real value out of the moment. Something else appears in the field of our attention and takes us in a new direction before we ever find the truth we seek. We need to put our egos aside and admit that we can't handle all of the information coming our way. We're not fast enough to think deeply about more than a few matters in a day. We need to be more like Napoleon and let our inboxes, messages, and voicemails fill up and focus on only the things we have already decided are important to us and take time to absorb everything else, or else we will absorb nothing at all. Intelligence operatives purposefully flood the enemy with information to hide the truth from them, yet we will actively do this to ourselves! Marcus Aurelius urged every person to ask themselves if what they were doing was really necessary.

Just like with food, you have an information diet. If you take in too much information, most of it bad, you will have a poor output. We need to clear our plates, in this case our minds, of everything that is bad for us.

KNOWLEDGE RETENTION TEST

1. Napoleon was your typical leader.

   True [ ]

   False [ ]

2. Napoleon insisted that his soldiers wake him with only bad news.

   True [ ]

   False [ ]

3. Truly successful people must make time to work through issues.

   True [ ]

   False [ ]

4. Our modern society makes it easy to deal with issues.

   True [ ]

   False [ ]

5. Constant distractions don't allow us to grow.

   True [ ]

   False [ ]

PREP WORK Q & A

1. How does our modern world stifle our ability to deal with issues?

_____

_____

_____

_____

_____

2. How can focusing on everything be detrimental?

_____

_____

_____

_____

_____

3. Why should we evaluate if everything we're doing is necessary?

_____

_____

_____

_____

_____

CHECKLIST

____Take a look at your typical day.

____Find places where you are overloading your mind with information.

____Consider how you can eliminate some of that information.

____Implement change to your day.

CHAPTER 4: EMPTY THE MIND

Shawn Green was being paid $14 million dollars per year by the LA Dodgers and he couldn't hit the ball. He was in a major rut and the media was scathing in its coverage of him. Upper-management at the Dodgers was beginning to lose confidence in Green's ability to turn things around. As most of us do when we're having a tough time at work, Green started to doubt himself and his doubts filled his mind.

In Major League Baseball, the ball leaves the pitcher's mound and travels towards home plate at just over ninety miles per hour on average. Hitting the ball is a difficult feat even if your mind is clear and focused. Imagine attempting to improve your ability to hit a small ball traveling that fast while your mind is clouded. Suddenly, a difficult task becomes near-impossible. Instead of giving in to the pressure or analyzing the art of hitting to death, Green started to focus on his Buddhism that had long been part of his life. He learned to clear his mind of doubt, fear, and chatter.

Green started to focus on the basic mechanics of his stance. He would repeat simple Buddhist sayings repeatedly to find a sense of focus. He would feel present at the place and let any doubts run rampant away from his attention. They were there but they weren't going to take over. The past didn't matter. The only thing that mattered was his stance and the mechanics of the swing. He hit the ball over the wall during the Dodger's rubber match against the Brewers. The slump was over! But now he felt himself getting excited and had to calm that voice as well. The feeling of excitement is just as dangerous as the nervousness of being in a slump. Both voices can lead you astray and away from the present moment.

So Green just emptied his mind and felt happy to be there. Without expectations of the future, he just focused on how he felt in the present and living out the moment. His teammates were going wild in the dugout. They were living in the past and future for him, so he decided to stay in the present where he was needed. Green went on to have one of the greatest single-game performances in the history of baseball. The crowd of almost 30,000 people rose from their feet in a standing ovation but Green continued to clear his mind.

Of course, expert opinion, thought, and specific knowledge is needed to be great in any field worth our effort. This knowledge is useless, however, if it's drowned out by the noise. That's why we must first empty our mind so what is truly important can surface. Like a clay cup that is formed around emptiness or the space between four walls, emptiness is essential to the value. Likewise, we must empty our mind to think deeply and clearly.

KNOWLEDGE RETENTION TEST

1. Shawn Green was a baseball player who couldn't hit the ball.

   True [ ]

   False [ ]

2. Shawn went to his Christian roots for help.

   True [ ]

   False [ ]

3. After slowing down his thoughts, Shawn was able to hit the ball out of the park.

   True [ ]

   False [ ]

4. Too many good or bad thoughts can take you from the present moment.

   True [ ]

   False [ ]

5. Too many thoughts don't allow you to think deeply.

   True [ ]

   False [ ]

PREP WORK Q & A

1. How did Shawn Green get out of his slump?

   _____

   _____

   _____

   _____

   _____

2. How can excitement also be detrimental?

   _____

   _____

   _____

   _____

   _____

3. Why is an empty mind important?

   _____

   _____

   _____

   _____

   _____

CHECKLIST

___Find something that you need to improve.

___Practice emptying your mind.

___Allow yourself to work through your situation with an empty mind.

___See how that empty mind can help you focus more.

CHAPTER 5: SLOW DOWN, THINK DEEPLY

Remember the show Mr. Rogers? Before Rogers would enter the scene and start singing his famous song about wanting you to be his neighbor, there would be a street light blinking yellow. It was fitting, as the entire show gave off the feeling of slowing down and just appreciating the moment we have with our neighbors. Rogers was bullied as a child and grew up with a sensitivity to others.

When we rush into action without understanding someone else, we often make a mistake. Earlier we learned how the Soviets jumped to conclusions about Kennedy and Kennedy did not return the favor, instead taking time to understand the intention of his adversary.

Philosophies throughout time reveal the same value. They relate the world to a muddy pool of water. You must remain patient and let the water settle before you can see things clearly. To be reactionary is to act without fully understanding what you're getting into. That's exactly what every episode of Mr. Rogers was about. He would slow things down and take the time to explain things and encourage the audience to do the same with everything they encountered.

It might seem like a contradiction to empty your mind but also think deeply. How can you think of nothing and think deeply at the same time? The point is to clear your mind of the everyday things getting in the way of thinking deeply. You must train yourself not to act on your initial thought or give it too much credence when you're trying to work through something difficult.

So, emptying your mind is the first step. Now, emptying the mind doesn't mean stopping yourself from having wandering thoughts. It's about letting those thoughts run their course. Let them zig and zag across each other until truly valuable patterns emerge. Then, when those valuable patterns emerge, you can compare those high-value patterns against each other. This is what is meant by deep thinking. Keeping a journal can help you accomplish this.

KNOWLEDGE RETENTION TEST

1. Mr. Rogers was bullied as a kid.

   True [ ]

   False [ ]

2. Most of Mr. Rogers focus on his show was about slowing down and not reacting.

   True [ ]

   False [ ]

3. It's impossible to empty your mind while also thinking deeply.

   True [ ]

   False [ ]

4. Allowing your thoughts to run through your mind isn't helpful.

   True [ ]

   False [ ]

5. Journaling can help process your thoughts.

   True [ ]

   False [ ]

PREP WORK Q & A

1. How is the world like muddy water?

_____

_____

_____

_____

_____

2. What did Mr. Rogers try to teach children?

_____

_____

_____

_____

_____

3. How can journaling help you think more clearly?

_____

_____

_____

_____

CHECKLIST

____Think of a time when you simply reacted.

____Consider how you would have responded if you had given it time.

____Work on thinking things through before immediately responding.

____Consider journaling to help with your thoughts.

CHAPTER 6: START JOURNALING

Anne Frank was given a journal for her thirteenth birthday. It actually was an autograph book but Anne saw it instead as an opportunity to confide in someone and find comfort. We now know just how much she would need a place to reflect during the remaining few years of her life. Just twenty-four days later she was forced into hiding in the attic above her family's warehouse.

Her father would later note that Anne didn't write every day. She would write when she was upset or had a specific problem. She also used it as an outlet to save her family from her outrage. She noted that her journal has more patience than people.

She commented that if everyone took the time to review their behavior at the end of each day, they would surely see their thoughts and try to do better when they woke up the next day. Over time, they could become truly remarkable through this self-optimization. She's right, as keeping a journal allows you to see yourself as a stranger without all of the biases of the ego. You can step off the ride that is the rollercoaster of life and redirect its course through reflection.

Some of the most accomplished people to ever live have kept journals. It's an intimidating list to research and you might think of yourself as a different type of individual from this esteemed list. But the most famous diarist or journal-keeper in history is Anne Frank and she was a hormonal teenager in an attic. If she can find the value in keeping a journal, do we really have an excuse?

A journal is a personal thing. What time of day, how often, and the structure of your journal writing should be entirely up to you. Find what works. However, don't skip over this tried and true method of reflection. There's no right way to start keeping a journal, the important part is to start and to keep in mind why you're doing it - to help 'empty' your mind, slow down, and think deeply.

KNOWLEDGE RETENTION TEST

1. Anne Frank wasn't a fan of journaling.

   True [ ]

   False [ ]

2. Anne Frank wrote in her journal every day.

   True [ ]

   False [ ]

3. A journal lets you see yourself as a stranger.

   True [ ]

   False [ ]

4. Many well known people have kept journals.

   True [ ]

   False [ ]

5. Journaling is most effective in the evening.

   True [ ]

   False [ ]

PREP WORK Q & A

1. How did journaling help Anne Frank?

2. _____

_____

_____

_____

_____

3. Why is journaling so helpful for people?

_____

_____

_____

_____

_____

4. What is the correct way to journal?

_____

_____

_____

_____

_____

CHECKLIST

___Understand why journaling is so important.

___Find a notebook you can use as a journal.

___Choose a time that you will be able to journal.

___Stick with it.

CHAPTER 7: CULTIVATE SILENCE

From an early age, composer John Cage was interested in silence. In a speech he delivered in high school, he argued that America should have a national day of silence to better understand one another.

Cage's interest in sound and silence would continue throughout his life. He felt the world was becoming too noisy. It's not that he was against noise in general. He enjoyed the ability to focus in on a specific sound or combination of sounds, but felt that sounds just became noise during our busy lives. In Cage's view, their specific beauty became lost in the chaos.

In his quest to understand silence, Cage visited the world's most soundproof room. Still, he told the engineer that he could still hear two sounds with his trained ear. The engineer informed him that they were from his own nervous system and his blood pumping through his body. Few of us will ever experience this level of silence.

Randall Stutman, a business advisor, took a survey of what high-level CEOs do in their downtime to unwind and think things through. He noticed a pattern in the answers (sailing, cycling, scuba-diving). All of these activities were relatively quiet. Specifically, there weren't any voices aside from the voice in your head. These were business professionals with a chaotic life and even though their free time involved moving, they were able to be still within their own minds. That was the key ingredient for focus.

Silence is a rare thing and it's never really achievable in a pure form. However, when you are able to find yourself in a place of relative quiet, take the time to think deeply about topics that are important to you. As you hear the ticking of the clock, remember that time for silence is key to hearing yourself think deeply about the things that matter.

KNOWLEDGE RETENTION TEST

1. The composer, John Cage, detested silence.

   True [ ]

   False [ ]

2. John Cage went on to try to understand full silence.

   True [ ]

   False [ ]

3. High level CEO's often have leisure activities that require silence.

   True [ ]

   False [ ]

4. Quiet is important for focus.

   True [ ]

   False [ ]

5. We can never really hear silence.

   True [ ]

   False [ ]

PREP WORK Q & A

1. Why did John Cage believe we should have a day of silence?

    _____

    _____

    _____

    _____

    _____

2. What do you hear in a soundproof room?

    _____

    _____

    _____

    _____

3. Why are quiet activities important?

    _____

    _____

    _____

    _____

CHECKLIST

____Think about your average day.

____List all the times you get to enjoy silence.

____Decide if you need more silence in your day.

____Find ways to be in the quiet.

CHAPTER 8: SEEK WISDOM

Socrates would often profess his lack of wisdom and that was actually a contributing factor to his wisdom. For centuries after his death, philosophers would note that Socrates understanding of how much he didn't know was a substantial factor in his ability to gain insight. In fact, Socrates would question things to the point that he would be annoying to most. He would question everyone's opinions and ask for evidence. He wanted to know just how minds worked and how the world was so he would ask every question he had. This line of questioning was so powerful and troubling that he would later be put to death for it.

Ancient Greeks, Buddhists, Christians, Muslims, Jews, and almost all groups of people live in cultures that respect wisdom. While their definitions might vary, the need for questioning and humility appears throughout all of them. Wisdom combines intelligence with the trial and error of experience which helps the thinker rise above their lazy peers. Since you're reading right now, it's evident that you are on your journey towards wisdom. Remember, there is not much difference between a person who doesn't read and a person who can't read.

Reading books is great but study must go beyond just reading. The founding of Stoicism can be traced back to when Zeno heard someone reading Socrates out loud. He asked directly where he can find a man like that which led him to his mentor Crates who helped shape Zeno as a person and thinker. Mentors help us overcome our faults and think more clearly. The Buddha also had more than one mentor and each helped shape the man we read about today. If these individuals needed mentors, then we can definitely benefit from them ourselves.

Seeking wisdom is not always easy. Sometimes it hurts. Wisdom takes hard work, sacrifice, and time. We must train our minds the same way we grow a muscle, stress testing it and rebuilding into something better. It's hard to think about what we don't know but that's exactly how we come to know something worthwhile. In your journey, you will learn things about the world and your own identity that will trouble you to your core. It's still much better than going through the world blind. Doubt is not our enemy. At the end of doubt is truth.

KNOWLEDGE RETENTION TEST

1. Socrates often admitted that he didn't know much.

   True [ ]

   False [ ]

2. Socrates wasn't interested in how the mind works.

   True [ ]

   False [ ]

3. Not many cultures respect wisdom.

   True [ ]

   False [ ]

4. All you must do is read.

   True [ ]

   False [ ]

5. Wisdom comes easily.

   True [ ]

   False [ ]

PREP WORK Q & A

1. What was Socrates like?

_____

_____

_____

_____

_____

2. How does a person gain wisdom?

_____

_____

_____

_____

_____

3. Why do we have to do more than just read?

_____

_____

_____

_____

_____

CHECKLIST

___Consider how Socrates understood what he didn't understand.

___Think about where you may be lacking understanding.

___Find where you can learn more about what you don't understand.

___Realize you will never completely understand.

CHAPTER 9: FIND CONFIDENCE, AVOID EGO

Philistia and Israel were locked in a terrible war three thousand years ago. There didn't seem to be an end to the struggle coming. Then, Goliath challenged any of the Israelites to one on one combat to end the conflict. He was huge and ego-driven but the Hebrew people were equally afraid. Not even Saul, the King of Israel, dared to step forward. Then, as you know, David stepped forward to accept the challenge.

David was so much smaller than Goliath, why has he so confident? He explained how he had chased down a bear and lion which had attacked their flock of sheep. He had a confidence based on evidence. He even went so far as to reject a suit of armor that he wasn't used to even when others urged for safety.

Goliath scoffed at David the way a bully would until his ego lost to David's confidence. We all knew how things ended for Goliath and it's a great reminder of the difference between losing with your ego and winning with confidence. The mind of the ego-driven man or woman is filled with manic delusions and insecurities. They make enemies and pick fights. They are selfish and complicated to deal with. Ego-driven people can be successful: Alexander the Great, Donald Trump, Howard Hughes, but would you want to trade places with them? They are constantly obsessed with the next battle. They need a stream of validation.

There's also the other side to the egomaniac: imposter syndrome. This is the all-too-common feeling that you're not good enough to be doing what you're doing. It's an anxiety that you haven't done enough and that you're not ready. What's the balance between the two? Confidence based on experience. It makes sense. It's objective. When you've prepared for something, you don't have to talk yourself into it and you won't talk yourself out of it. Ulysses S. Grant's father was an egomaniac but his mother was calm, cool, and collected even during trying times. Confident people have a clear understanding of what matters most in the moment and do not let fear change their approach. They don't feel a need to create a false appearance. They don't need or expect praise or glory and this is exactly how they're able to obtain respect. A confident person seeks the truth and to act in accordance with the truth and they are fine with adjusting their position. They aren't burdened by the additional responsibility of caring for their ego.

We all fall somewhere on this spectrum between egomaniac, confidence, and imposter syndrome. It's important to identify where you are so you can move towards the center (and being centered). Confidence means being content even when things go wrong. If you're a mess when things aren't going your way, life will be much more difficult. It will be like a living hell. No one is perfect; it's okay to be insecure or a bit egotistical. Just be sure to know when this is the case and make an effort not to feed into your ego and insecurities. Just let them be as you continue your business.

KNOWLEDGE RETENTION TEST

1. David won against Goliath because of his ego.

   True [ ]

   False [ ]

2. People who are driven by their ego are calm.

   True [ ]

   False [ ]

3. Egomaniacs need validation.

   True [ ]

   False [ ]

4. Confident people don't let fear move them.

   True [ ]

   False [ ]

5. Only rich people are egomaniacs.

   True [ ]

   False [ ]

PREP WORK Q & A

1. What is imposter syndrome?

   _____

   _____

   _____

   _____

   _____

2. How did David defeat Goliath?

   _____

   _____

   _____

   _____

   _____

3. Why should you figure out if you're an egomaniac, confident or living with imposter syndrome?

   _____

   _____

   _____

   _____

   _____

CHECKLIST

___Understand the signs of your ego.

___Consider if you often let your ego be in control.

___Determine if you have imposter syndrome.

___Find ways to move from fear to confidence.

CHAPTER 10: LET GO

Awa Kenzo was an archery master. He taught students the art of archery but barely ever taught them any mechanic archery technique. He instead taught them to let go of their expectations. He told them about a special state they could achieve if they simply let go of the expectation of any outcome and just focused on shooting for its own sake. This was an ego-less state that was about the input and not the output. It was a *still* state. He argued that a will that was too willful would simply get in your way.

But wait, aren't we supposed to be driven by purpose? Isn't this what creates successful people? It all felt a bit contradictory to many of his students and it might feel contradictory to you now. Let's slow down and think about it. Have you ever wanted something so bad that you're too busy wanting it to actually get it? The same applies to archery, golf, and many other things in life. If you try to go too fast you will end up being slower. As modern marksman like to put it, slow is smooth, smooth is fast. Sure, we need to learn technique. However, to improve, we often need to loosen up a bit. To let go of that need of control. Perhaps you've heard the phrase 'let loose'. This is a type of focus that embodies confidence. Think of a great sports performance you've seen lately. Did you find the athlete to be tense or loose?

Kenzo argued that the technical tricks each practitioner used ultimately lead nowhere. He felt they were no improvement over letting go the most that you could. Things that require more steps than archery show the same thing. A student goes into a class with expectations and previous knowledge which they want to use to force themselves to the front of the line, skipping the necessary series of moments and thinking of the outcome.

Kenzo would have his students shoot at large bales of hay with no defined target. After months of doing so, he would finally announce that the students would now fire at a target. If they missed wildly, he would tell them to keep shooting as if nothing had happened. If they hit the bullseye, he would tell them the exact same thing. He wanted his students to get lost in the process of shooting and offered them no additional instruction. He wanted them to surrender themselves to the practice.

The more we forget about the end result, the easier it is to achieve. The more creative and productive we become. We must let go to hit difficult targets.

KNOWLEDGE RETENTION TEST

1. Awa Kenzo taught his students the mechanics of archery.

   True [ ]

   False [ ]

2. Kenzo taught his students to let go of expectations.

   True [ ]

   False [ ]

3. A confident athlete is tense.

   True [ ]

   False [ ]

4. Working slowly and confidently helps a person learn faster.

   True [ ]

   False [ ]

5. Letting go helps you achieve more.

   True [ ]

   False [ ]

PREP WORK Q & A

1. Why is it better to go slow?

_____

_____

_____

_____

_____

2. What does it mean to "let loose"?

_____

_____

_____

_____

3. Why did Kenzo not give his students a target?

_____

_____

_____

_____

CHECKLIST

___Think about something you've struggled to learn.

___Determine if you were trying too hard.

___Decide if you could "let loose" when learning.

___Try again without a goal in mind.

Congrats, you're working hard so you've earned a little fun break. You'll notice 3 such fun breaks within this workbook, each with a different difficulty level. All of the words below should be familiar as they are taken from this book. Give your brain a mini vacation then jump back into learning. (Answers on next page)

Find the following words in the puzzle.
Words are hidden → ↓ and ↘ .

ABRAMOVIC   KENNEDY   RYANHOLIDAY
AGGRESSIVE   KRUSHCHEV   SOLITUDE
BUDDHIST   MARINA   STILLNESS
CUBAN   MONK   TRANQUILITY
HOSTILITY   RUSSIANS

FUN BREAK 1 OF 3 ANSWER SHEET

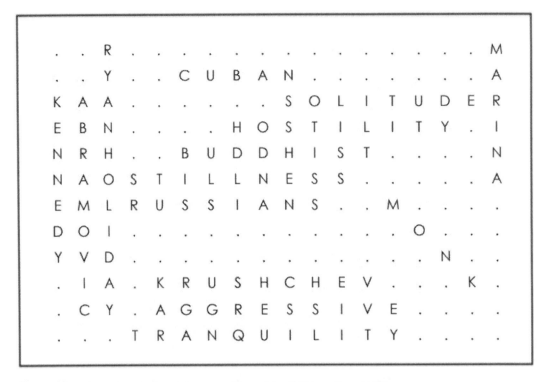

```
. . R . . . . . . . . . . . . . M
. . Y . . C U B A N . . . . . . A
K A A . . . . . . S O L I T U D E R
E B N . . . . H O S T I L I T Y . I
N R H . . B U D D H I S T . . . . N
N A O S T I L L N E S S . . . . . A
E M L R U S S I A N S . . M . . . .
D O I . . . . . . . . . . . O . . .
Y V D . . . . . . . . . . . . N . .
. I A . K R U S H C H E V . . . K .
. C Y . A G G R E S S I V E . . . .
. . . T R A N Q U I L I T Y . . . .
```

Word directions and start points are formatted: (Direction, X, Y)

ABRAMOVIC (S,2,3)   KENNEDY (S,1,3)   RYANHOLIDAY (S,3,1)
AGGRESSIVE (E,5,11)   KRUSHCHEV (E,5,10)   SOLITUDE (E,10,3)
BUDDHIST (E,6,5)   MARINA (S,18,1)   STILLNESS (E,4,6)
CUBAN (E,6,2)   MONK (SE,14,7)   TRANQUILITY (E,4,12)
HOSTILITY (E,8,4)   RUSSIANS (E,4,7)

CHAPTER 11: ON TO WHAT'S NEXT

We only have limited time to reach our goals and time is far too precious to waste on noise. The buzzing of the crowd leads us astray. The wisdom we seek is buried so deep that we must be able to see what most people cannot see. So, we have to empty our minds, sit with our journals, and be as still as we can to find the truth we seek.

When we are able to find this level of stillness, we become near superhuman. We surprise ourselves with our clarity, capabilities, and pure feelings of joy. Those feelings are usually all too temporary, aren't they? Why aren't we able to stay in this form for longer?

Our mind seeks stillness but impulses are its enemy. We enjoy these moments and then we are pulled in another direction from external stimulus and internal cravings. Short moments of clarity and stillness are not on our agenda. That's a glimpse at what we're capable of but we can do much better than that. It's going to require much more work to get there but it will be worth it in the long run. Those moments of brilliance will extend manifold. We must align our bodies with our desires to extend our existence in stillness. In truth, our mind, spirit, and body are all at war with one another. We've discussed the mind and now we are on to our souls.

PART II: SPIRIT

CHAPTER 12: THE DOMAIN OF THE SOUL

Tiger Woods hit a birdie on the 18th hole of the US Open in 2008. The act forced an 18-hole showdown against Rocco Mediate into a sudden-death round. Tiger would hit yet another birdie and win the Open for the third time in his career. Alone, it would be an astounding feat on the June day. What made it immensely more impressive was the Tiger was playing on a torn ACL and a leg broken in two places. The crowd had no idea about the extent of his injuries. After the win, he had to take leave from the game to have knee surgery.

Within six months his wife found out about his mistress and attacked him with a golf club as he crashed his vehicle trying to escape. He laid sprawled out on their lawn, still, without his consciousness. His sex scandals then began to pour out. Pornstars, waitresses, even 21-year-old family friends. His life evolved into a tabloid mess filled with shame. It would be over ten years before he would win another major.

On the surface and in his sport, Woods had absolute stillness and discipline. Underneath was a raging and insatiable sea which threatened to drown him. Woods could overcome his opponents on the golf course but he couldn't face his own demons.

The chaos was started early in his life. His father, Earl, came home from his military tour in Vietnam with a new wife and child which he failed to mention to his current wife and children who were waiting for him at home. Earl Woods was not excited about being a father again and this is the context which Tiger was born into. Instead of playing with other kids, Tiger Woods was hitting golf balls at two years old. It might seem like too much to some but it's also what enabled him to be one of the best players the game has ever seen, if not the best.

His father would harass him starting at seven-years-old to focus his concentration. He was brutal. He would throw things at him, get in his view, call him the n word. Anything to try and break his concentration while he played so he could learn to ignore it. His father even gave him the cold safety word of 'enough' to utter if things ever got too much for him. Tiger never used it and the two would joke about the 'e-word' as something quitters would use. This combination turned Tiger into a winning golfer but not a very happy person.

KNOWLEDGE RETENTION TEST

1. In 2008, Tiger Woods played with a leg broken in two places.

   True [ ]

   False [ ]

2. Tiger Woods could be calm on the golf course and in his personal life.

   True [ ]

   False [ ]

3. Tiger Woods never played golf again.

   True [ ]

   False [ ]

4. Tiger was pushed to be a great golfer by his father.

   True [ ]

   False [ ]

5. Tiger's father desensitized him to distractions which helped him be a better golfer.

   True [ ]

   False [ ]

PREP WORK Q & A

1. How did Tiger Woods become a golf legend?

   _____

   _____

   _____

   _____

   _____

2. How did Tiger's father influence his life?

   _____

   _____

   _____

   _____

   _____

3. How did he gain his focus?

   _____

   _____

   _____

   _____

   _____

CHECKLIST

___Think about places in life you've lost focus.

___Determine how you might start to focus more.

___Understand how important focus is.

___Work everyday on your focus.

CHAPTER 13: CHOOSE VIRTUE

Emperor Marcus Aurelius authored a list of qualities that he believed a person should have to increase their character and effectiveness in the world. He urged sanity, cooperation, and being straightforward (among others). I'm sure you can think of many others you would add to your own list. There's one idea, however, that encapsulates all others: virtue.

A virtue is the highest Earthly good that a single person could achieve. Virtue is not an exclusively religious quality but one dictated by social and moral wellness. Eastern and Western societies have both historically favored virtuous individuals and Confucius would have found some commonality in Marcus Aurelius' pursuit of virtue.

Now, it might seem like the pursuit of virtue is for the approval of those around you, a bit of an elitist goal. However, to live with virtue is to live with meaning. There is nothing more empty than a life lived without meaning. Therefore, determining virtue and living by it has its own value independent of others. To be virtuous is to know why you are acting which gives a feeling of certainty even if you aren't sure what your outcomes will be. It's a source of inspiration to draw upon even the most trying times.

There are different virtues for different situations. When we are tasked with taking on something a bit scary, we can call upon the virtues of strength and courage to bring us to success. When we are about to have a difficult conversation with a loved one, kindness and empathy will better suit the situation.

The highest virtues have not been universally determined and are specific to each individual. That's why you need to sit down and ask yourself what is most important *to you*. What is your highest value? What inspires you? In the depths of you, when it really comes down to it, what matters most?

Confucius wrote that a gentleman remains calm, cool, and collected but the person who is petty is constantly worried. He also wrote that living in virtue will attract the company of others who live by the same virtues.

Seneca was the advisor to Nero. He taught Nero the virtues and said that judgment based on virtue was the highest good. He believed that wealth corrupts and that kindness was the key to life. However, Seneca's actions did not match his teachings. He accumulated mass wealth and helped the cruel Emperor Nero. Eventually, his ways caught up to him when Nero forced him to kill himself.

So, it's one thing to have virtues and another to live by them. We can't give up on our virtues when it is expedient because it will hurt us in the long run. When others give in and abandon their virtues, you must be still.

KNOWLEDGE RETENTION TEST

1. Being virtuous is the highest good any person can gain.

   True [ ]

   False [ ]

2. To live with virtue gives your life meaning.

   True [ ]

   False [ ]

3. Virtue is a religious quality.

   True [ ]

   False [ ]

4. There are different virtues for different situations.

   True [ ]

   False [ ]

5. Having virtues and living by them are two different things.

   True [ ]

   False [ ]

PREP WORK Q & A

1. What is a virtue?

    _____

    _____

    _____

    _____

    _____

2. Why are there different virtues for different situations?

    _____

    _____

    _____

    _____

    _____

3. Why do virtues change depending on the person?

    _____

    _____

    _____

    _____

    _____

CHECKLIST

___Understand what a virtue is.

___Decide what virtues are important to you.

___Find where you may need to apply these virtues.

___Choose to live by those virtues.

CHAPTER 14: HEAL THE INNER CHILD

Leonardo Davinci often acted childish. He loved being creative and caused a bit of trouble in his adult life. However, there was a dark side to his actual childhood. He was born the bastard son to a noble family. Even though his father helped him secure an apprenticeship in the arts, he always felt distant. He passively did not have a will which was a way of disinheriting Leonardo. Some biographers argue that in most of Leonardo's works of art was a child's need for fatherly love and acceptance.

Whenever a patron would slight Leonardo or give less than he wanted, he would become extremely irritable and abandon the work half finished. He was sensitive, making him inflexible when dealing with others he desired full cooperation from.

Many of us are carrying baggage from our childhood. Perhaps we are resentful that we weren't raised correctly. Perhaps we weren't given the tools needed to be successful. We might carry these wounds with us and it might negatively affect our relationships. We should see this as a relief, as our negative aspects are not our fault. However, it is our responsibility to change things. We can't carry on this way.

When we want to protect the wounded child underneath, we tend to create monsters. They are designed to help us deal with the world but they only make life more difficult. They end up making things more stressful. Judd Apatow used to react to the perceived unfair treatment of studios imposing restrictions on his movies in a childish, rebellious manner. Over time and with therapy, he learned to see the exchanges as adult conversations about the creative process. This lowered the amount of stress at work, increasing stillness.

We have to take the time to think about our specific wounds from the past. We need to stop hurting others with our pain and making things worse for ourselves. Deep reflection about things from our past can help us better deal with them. We need to be better for ourselves and for everyone we meet.

KNOWLEDGE RETENTION TEST

1. Leonardo DaVinci often acted childish.

   True [ ]

   False [ ]

2. DaVinci had childhood trauma that caused him to act out.

   True [ ]

   False [ ]

3. Our childhood trauma is only for others to fix.

   True [ ]

   False [ ]

4. Negative reactions are because others have wronged us.

   True [ ]

   False [ ]

5. Deep reflection can help us heal our wounds.

   True [ ]

   False [ ]

PREP WORK Q & A

1. How did DaVinci's childhood affect his relationships with others?

   _____

   _____

   _____

   _____

   _____

2. How does childhood baggage affect us day to day?

   _____

   _____

   _____

   _____

   _____

3. How can we work through our personal traumas?

   _____

   _____

   _____

   _____

   _____

CHECKLIST

___Understand childhood trauma.

___Evaluate your own childhood traumas.

___See how it's affected your reaction to others.

___Take steps to change your reactions.

CHAPTER 15: BEWARE DESIRE

Earlier, we discussed how stillness helped President John F. Kennedy achieve greatness. However, he was human like the rest of us and had deeper issues which disturbed that same stillness. For instance, his father often would bring home mistresses at night when he was a child. He would even bring them along on family vacations. His father instilled in him the need to truly hate his adversaries, which raised the level of anger in the household.

Kennedy's sex drive got him in trouble time and time again, but each time he got away with it. This only made his habit even worse. Former lovers would say that it was purely physical for him and he barely seemed to care who he was having sex with. In one instance of 'too much information', Kennedy admitted to Britain's prime minister that he would get headaches if he went too many days without having sex (it was actually just a couple of days). Coupled with Kennedy's back problems, one can assume that sex wasn't even that physically pleasurable for him. Even during the Cuba Missile Crisis, he met with a nineteen year old girl in a hotel room. While the world was at the brink of nuclear war, he was cheating on his wife with some strange young girl. If that doesn't sound like stillness, that's because it isn't. It's exploits of a man with a wounded soul.

We might be quick to condemn Kennedy but we all have desires which we can barely control. The desire to be with a beautiful woman, or to have nice things, or that next sugar rush. We all have impulses that we give in to when we know there's a better way. If you are a slave to your urges, do you really have free will? Think of the seven deadly sins. How many affect your mind? A person consumed with envy, for instance, cannot think clearly. Epicurus once taught that sex has never benefited any man and if it hasn't injured him that it's a miracle.

Most of the impulses that we have are irrational desires. We have to really think about and dissect them before we act on them. We have to ask how they will benefit us if we act on them. Stillness is not about being a saint or never enjoying your life, but it will give you the chance to think about how much power you want to give to your desires.

KNOWLEDGE RETENTION TEST

1. Kennedy had childhood trauma just like everyone else.

   True [ ]

   False [ ]

2. Kennedy cheated on his wife because he could.

   True [ ]

   False [ ]

3. Everyone has impulses they struggle to control.

   True [ ]

   False [ ]

4. People do bad things in order to hurt others.

   True [ ]

   False [ ]

5. The seven deadly sins are mostly mental.

   True [ ]

   False [ ]

PREP WORK Q & A

1. How did Kennedy's childhood affect him in his adulthood?

   _____

   _____

   _____

   _____

   _____

2. How are we all slaves to our urges?

   _____

   _____

   _____

   _____

   _____

3. How are most impulses irrational desires?

   _____

   _____

   _____

   _____

   _____

CHECKLIST

___Realize how our childhood affects our adulthood.

___Reflect on how your childhood has shaped who you have become.

___Decide if there are things you would like to change.

___Understand why you do those things in the first place.

CHAPTER 16: ENOUGH

Kurt Vonnegut and Joseph Heller, both accomplished authors, were once at a party together in a fancy community. Kurt asked Joseph how it felt to know that their host made more money in a single day than their novels would make in their lifetimes. Joe responded that he had something that the billionaire would never have, *enough.*

Having enough frees you from the insecurity of comparing yourself from others, the desire to constantly need more, sometimes enough can be more than enough. The content you get from enough can be everything. However, it's not something you can just say. It's something you need to work on. Being content with enough is deeply spiritual business and requires a process in most of us.

Whatever it is you're chasing will likely not bring you the peace you seek. Once you achieve your goal or you get the objects that you desire, something else will take their place. It will never be enough until you are content with enough. Some level of desire is healthy and needed but it can also run rampant and be difficult to contain. If you can't learn to appreciate life as it is, you will never experience a feeling of stillness. You will be in a constant state of motion attempting to reach some new state of being. Some of the best philosophies on the subject come from the East, where it is taught to accept things as they are. When we are obsessed with what may be in the future, we lose sight of what is right in front of us. You have to ask what outcomes you really want more of.

Instead of more things, more money, and more accomplishments, is it possible that you would be better off with more peace? More stillness?

KNOWLEDGE RETENTION TEST

1. Feeling like you have enough is as easy as saying it.

    True [ ]

    False [ ]

2. You must appreciate life as it is to feel stillness.

    True [ ]

    False [ ]

3. It's important to never be satisfied with where you are.

    True [ ]

    False [ ]

4. The East taught us to accept things are they are.

    True [ ]

    False [ ]

5. The key is knowing how to have more peace in your life rather than more things.

    True [ ]

    False [ ]

PREP WORK Q & A

1. Why do some people never have enough?

_____

_____

_____

_____

_____

2. How does being content give you more?

_____

_____

_____

_____

_____

3. Why should you appreciate life as it is?

_____

_____

_____

_____

_____

CHECKLIST

____Think about your goals and desires.

____Decide when you would have "enough".

____Think about what that would actually mean for you.

____Understand that more peace may be what you need instead.

CHAPTER 17: BATHE IN BEAUTY

Peter was a young Jewish boy that Anne Frank shared the attic with those two long years they were forced into hiding. There was a particular spot she liked to lie down with him and look out the window at the world which they could not venture into. The openness of the outside, even while only being able to view it, was enough to put them into a tranquil dream-like state. The world was at war and Hitler had put millions of their fellow Jewish people to death while thousands more starved in the camps. Their lives were forced to the shadows. Yet, even then, they were able to find these moments of peace and bask in the glory of nature. She wrote in her diary that she could not be sad as long as the sun was shining and the sky was clear.

These moments where we can step outside of our worries are available to us whenever we seek them. There is always some beautiful part of the world to gaze upon even during the darkest moments. We just have to be open to seeing these wonders.

There were once two farm hands working for a zen master and his farm. They asked him to teach them his ways so they might also experience zen. He said that when they finished their work they could find him and learn. They worked hard throughout the day and then found him. For the lesson, he simply outstretched his arms as he sat and took in the setting sun on the farm. Did the zen master trick the boys? Not at all. Basking in the glory of a growing crop after a hard days work *is* zen.

Finding the beauty in superficial objects or becoming too obsessed with the ugliness of the world will make anyone bitter. Both views make the viewer ugly. However, to find the beauty in all things creates a more peaceful individual and makes way for a peaceful life. That's the job of the poet and philosopher, to study the awe of reality. Don't let it escape you. Bathe in the beauty.

KNOWLEDGE RETENTION TEST

1. Anne Frank once wrote that she couldn't be sad while the sun was shining.

   True [ ]

   False [ ]

2. Sometimes it's impossible to step out of our worries.

   True [ ]

   False [ ]

3. Anne Frank couldn't even look outside.

   True [ ]

   False [ ]

4. There is always something beautiful to focus on instead of our pain.

   True [ ]

   False [ ]

5. Things can bring you happiness.

   True [ ]

   False [ ]

PREP WORK Q & A

1. How can we step outside of our worries?

_____

_____

_____

_____

_____

2. How can hard work bring you zen?

_____

_____

_____

_____

_____

3. Why is finding beauty in all things important?

_____

_____

_____

_____

_____

CHECKLIST

___Think about your goals in life.

___Decide which are simply about things.

___Reflect on how the work to get there is just as important.

___Begin to shift your perspective on what's important.

CHAPTER 18: ACCEPT A HIGHER POWER

Over its history, the hardest step for alcoholics in AA is the acceptance of a higher power. One might think that this is because of the increased secularism of the world. However, the inability to accept a higher power has stayed rather steady and has been an issue even at a time where most alcoholics were already religious. The problem is that it's difficult for an addict, or anyone, to admit someone or something else can help them.

The step isn't about religion or God. It's about the ability to surrender yourself to a process. Something greater than you. That's what you're putting your faith into. Remember, earlier we learned about letting go. This is the ultimate form of letting go. It's not about God but it's about admitting that *you're not God and you're not in control.* This isn't just true for addicts, it's true for all of us in an ultimate sense. We can't control everything and we are bound to get in our own way the more we try to control. AA doesn't mention a specific religion. Whatever you choose to believe in is up to you, as long as you believe it's stronger than the sum of your parts. You can even believe that the force is just bad luck.

People are quick to think of a judgmental or obsessive God. Epicurus rejected this idea. There have been many forms of Gods across different cultures but it doesn't seem to align that God would want people to be afraid. God's most common feature is that he, she, or it is a guide to help you through life. Should we look on all these ancient people as ignorant? Do you think a Buddhist monk would want to trade places with you for wealth, technology, or science?

The point is to override the constant authority of your mind. To let a stronger force, or even just the idea of it, into your heart to slow your mind and give you a break from the stress. You might not be ready to do that right now but you should know that the option of accepting something greater than yourself is always open to you.

KNOWLEDGE RETENTION TEST

1. The hardest step for many in AA is apologizing to others.

   True [ ]

   False [ ]

2. The ultimate form of letting go is trusting in God.

   True [ ]

   False [ ]

3. Trying to control your life is the best way to get your life in order.

   True [ ]

   False [ ]

4. Many think God is judgmental.

   True [ ]

   False [ ]

5. Letting go to a higher power helps relieve stress in your life.

   True [ ]

   False [ ]

PREP WORK Q & A

1. What is so hard for many people to do?

_____

_____

_____

_____

_____

2. Do you have to believe in God to let go?

_____

_____

_____

_____

_____

3. Would God want people to be fearful?

_____

_____

_____

_____

_____

CHECKLIST

____Consider how you feel about God.

____Understand that God doesn't want you to feel fear.

____Learn to trust in a higher power.

____Understand that letting go can relieve some of your stress.

CHAPTER 19: ENTER RELATIONSHIPS

Johnny Cash's first marriage fell apart in the 1960's. He moved from California to Tennessee. His new home was giant and wedged between a hill and a beautiful lake. He paced across the home anxiously. He couldn't shake the feeling that he had forgotten something. He thought of what he might have left back home when it hit him. He was by the lake bed when he realized he needed his daughter Rosanne there with him. The house could not be a home without her. He called her name until he collapsed on the ground.

We can't include our deepest relationships with our notion of letting go. There's a level of love and commitment which goes beyond the purely transactional. Relationships aren't the same as base desires or distractions, not the ones that should really matter like Cash's relationship with his daughter. Yes, we just talked about a Buddhist monk not wanting to trade places with you but if you have a plethora of healthy relationships - that might be the one thing someone who has taken a vow of solitude should envy (of course, they have probably transcended envy). We are nothing without our relationships and we aren't really in a good relationship unless we are selfless. This is what allows us to really see and appreciate the other person and not just use them to our own selfish needs. What would the point be of obtaining stillness if you didn't have anyone to love or be loved by? Why develop this power if you can't share it with those around you.

Even masters of stillness struggle with this. Marina Abramovic, whose performance art we covered earlier, stated that she remained single and without children because she didn't have enough energy to perform and have a family. She is wrong.

Madame Curie was a love skeptic too until she met her husband Pierre. They fell in love, married, and won the Nobel Prize together. John Stuart Mills cited his wife as the inspiration for all of his great writing. Angela Merkel, the German chancellor, has been supported by her husband through her entire career. Stillness is even better when its pursuit is shared (ever do a group yoga class?). Relationships are difficult but there are countless examples of sharing your life and still succeeding at the highest of levels.

We are not our full selves without others. We might deny it rationally but we will feel it in our depths that something is wrong, like Cash shouting his daughter's name on the banks of the strange lake. We need to let other people in.

KNOWLEDGE RETENTION TEST

1. Johnny Cash realized after his divorce that he needed to be alone.

   True [ ]

   False [ ]

2. Deep relationships don't count when it comes to letting go.

   True [ ]

   False [ ]

3. You don't need to share your life with anyone in order to be happy.

   True [ ]

   False [ ]

4. Relationships can help you become your full self.

   True [ ]

   False [ ]

5. Love and commitment on some level is more than just transactional.

   True [ ]

   False [ ]

PREP WORK Q & A

1. How are relationships different than base desires?

_____

_____

_____

_____

_____

2. How can sharing your life help you?

_____

_____

_____

_____

_____

3. Why should you take a long look at your relationships?

_____

_____

_____

_____

CHECKLIST

___Understand that there is a difference between base desire and relationships.

___Look at the relationships in your life and see how they affect you.

___Eliminate those that don't bring you closer to the person you want to be.

___Understand everyone needs relationships with others on some level.

CHAPTER 20: CONQUER YOUR ANGER

When Michael Jordan was inducted into the Basketball Hall of Fame, his speech wasn't what people expected. He discussed every slight he had during his career. He talked about the man who had made the team in high school when he was cut. But Leroy Smith didn't lead to Michael being cut, did he? In fact, Michael wasn't cut from that team. They both tried out and the underclassmen wasn't chosen. That's pretty normal. But it 'cut' Michael deeply and he carried it with him all those years. Leroy was 6'7 at the time and Michael wasn't even 6 feet yet. Who would you have chosen as a coach? Instead of being rational or a team player, Michael chose to remain mad about it.

Things grew more and more awkward for the audience as Michael discussed kicking Pat Riley, a head coach, out of a hotel that he wanted to stay in. Michael let the audience know that he didn't invite the Bull's GM to the ceremony because he once implied that teams win championships together, which Michael saw as diminishing his own ability. Jordan's goal was to prove that you can overcome all doubters. He accomplished this to some degree but also showed how ugly it can be when you let anger fester and then blow up everywhere; it's not a pretty sight.

Was anger the necessary fuel for Jordan to be successful? It's hard to say. Wayne Gretsky seems to win without being too upset. The same goes for Tom Brady. Is Michael's anger, instead of fuel, the one ingredient that kept him from enjoying his success? Richard Nixon said that haters only win when you hate them back, and that the hatred will destroy you. He then proved his own words to be true as he self-destructed.

Desire is something we need to watch out for. Anger, on the other hand, is something we must conqueror. No one who is angry is happy. Anger hurts everyone around us. Replace your anger with love and purpose.

KNOWLEDGE RETENTION TEST

1. Michael Jordan surprised people with his speech when he was inducted into the Hall of Fame.

   True [ ]

   False [ ]

2. Anger was a big push for Michael Jordan.

   True [ ]

   False [ ]

3. Anger can help you realize your dreams.

   True [ ]

   False [ ]

4. Anger is a useful tool that doesn't harm you.

   True [ ]

   False [ ]

5. Anger can lead to happiness.

   True [ ]

   False [ ]

PREP WORK Q & A

1. Why was Michael Jordan angry?

   _____

   _____

   _____

   _____

   _____

2. How does anger work against you?

   _____

   _____

   _____

   _____

   _____

3. Explain why anger should be controlled.

   _____

   _____

   _____

   _____

CHECKLIST

___Identify the ways anger has ruled you.

___Realize that anger doesn't have a place in your life.

___Think of ways you can help release your anger.

___Work on letting your anger go.

CHAPTER 21: ALL IS ONE

Edgar Mitchell was hurled into space in 1971. Thousands of miles above the Earth's surface, he looked down with a profound new sense of the world. His perspective changed figuratively as it changed literally. He felt that he shared a single consciousness with everyone on Earth. He felt the need to change things for the better. He felt that the bickering on Earth felt so insignificant in view of all the glory before him all those miles up. Differences between races, nations, and religions just didn't seem important. He just felt connected to everyone. He wanted to grab all the politicians down below and drag them to space with him to see exactly what he was seeing. Not out of anger but out of the new sense of calmness he felt towards existence. He wanted everyone to be able to feel that stillness and act accordingly. He knew that we're all in this *together*.

Whether you get it from the careful use of a drug, meditation, or a religious experience, the realization that everything is connected is transformative. The Greeks had a name for this connectivity: *sympatheia*. It is the idea that everyone should be respected for the part that they play in the whole of humanity and the world as a single system. The utility in this comes from understanding that not only are you connected to those who you love or share values with but you are also connected to those you despise. Those who cheat in life. Those who cheat on their spouses. You can feel a level of patience with them because they are part of the same system you are - they have just manifested in a different form.

Think of someone or something that you love dearly and remember that everyone out there feels that way about someone. Everyone has felt that warmth. It's a shared experience. The bad feelings, too, are shared by all of us. We are all made out of the same star dust (or nuclear waste if you'd rather put it that way). We share this planet with a billion other people. True joy is enjoying their victories and happiness as much as you enjoy your own. That's when you are truly free. When we forget this, we forget ourselves.

KNOWLEDGE RETENTION TEST

1. The astronaut Edgar Mitchell was transformed by the view of the Earth from space.

   True [ ]

   False [ ]

2. The things that divide us are very important.

   True [ ]

   False [ ]

3. Realizing we are all connected can be transformative.

   True [ ]

   False [ ]

4. Even those who do bad are still connected to us in some way.

   True [ ]

   False [ ]

5. Nothing we can do can change another person's life.

   True [ ]

   False [ ]

PREP WORK Q & A

1. How was Edgar Mitchell changed by his experience in space?

_____

_____

_____

_____

_____

2. How are we all connected?

_____

_____

_____

_____

_____

3. Why is feeling connected to everyone else important?

_____

_____

_____

_____

_____

CHECKLIST

____Consider how the people in your life affect you.

____Think about how you may affect others you know.

____Understand that even people you don't like have people that love them.

____Think about how important every person is in this world.

CHAPTER 22: ON TO WHAT'S NEXT

What we need is often right in front of us but it's not something we can see with the naked eye. As the children's story *The Little Prince* teaches us, we need our heart to see it. Our journey started with mental clarity. The mind and the soul work together to bring mental clarity but its the heart working with the soul that can reveal the most important things in life, things that go beyond simple rationalizing.

Tears and peeling onions go together, as you might have experienced. You can think of this metaphor as you peel back the onion that is the layers of your emotions. It's really in these small details of balancing the emotional state of the body that can create an efficient machine. You probably heard the term 'gut feeling'. This is apt because your soul is connected to your body. You can't optimize one without the other. You must take care of your soul to cultivate the body and you must move well to be still.

A tired, overworked, or malnourished body can't be considered completely still and will negatively affect all aspects of your life. Being overworked makes you susceptible to your worst vices. Being lazy creates an ugliness in your soul. You must work to avoid both of these extremes.

Life is far too difficult to let our mind and soul be weakened through a soft constitution. We must take care of and strengthen our bodies if we are to have a successful life. The body anchors the mind and soul.

PART III: BODY

CHAPTER 23: THE DOMAIN OF THE BODY

Winston Churchill had a relatively busy life. He saw combat at 21 years of age and wrote a book about it shortly after. The book went on to be a bestseller. He was elected to public office by the age of 26 and would serve in Government for the next 65 years. He wrote dozens of books, millions of words, and painted hundreds of paintings. He gave dozens of memorial speeches. You might remember that he helped save the free world from the Nazis. He spent his final years fighting communism.

He lived a long 90 years. His life started during the end of the British imperial century and traversed into the space age. Could someone who fit so much experience into their life be considered calm and still? Oddly enough, yes.

Paul Johnson was a biographer of Churchill and discussed Churchill's balance between work and rest. Johnson first met Churchill when he was a young lad and asked Churchill to what he attributed his success, and he detailed that it was the conservation of energy which helped him succeed. Don't stand up until you have to. Don't sit down if you can lie down. This allowed Churchill to be ready for any task without burning out. When he had nothing to do, he built up his energy for the next task that would surely spring up soon enough. If he was active during his down time he would have very little energy left for the battle. There are many somewhat conflicting philosophies of how to live a good life: Be disciplined, seek pleasure, glorify God, relax, keep working.

In truth, the best of us incorporate all of these philosophies with a healthy balance. That's what Churchill did. He worked with his hands in art and bricklaying, was a politician, a soldier, serious when needed, and a jokester. Balance! You would think that Churchill was born with a strong constitution to carry out such a strong will. This is not the case. Churchill was a weak child with severe physical limitations. He once remarked that he barely had enough energy to be tired. However, his spirit allowed him to extend his control of his body to get done what needed to get done. He was strategic. We learned what we did in an earlier chapter: that greatness was better sought with a companion. He married his fiancé Clementine and called it his life's greatest achievement.

He thought out his entire life to keep improving himself. His famous lines were actually quite rehearsed. At the end of every night he would take on the role of judge and try himself; did he really accomplish anything worthwhile during the day? If not, he would force himself to improve. It wasn't a frantic uneasiness or insecurity. It was a confident movement towards progress and an objective view of himself.

There are traits we will need if we are to do half us much as Churchill in our lives: we must rest, seek out time to be alone, develop a routine to stick to, evaluate ourselves, rise above physical shortcomings, and be a part of something bigger than just ourselves.

KNOWLEDGE RETENTION TEST

1. Winston Churchill wrote a book at 25 that went on to be a bestseller.

    True [ ]

    False [ ]

2. Churchill said that conserving his energy was part of his success.

    True [ ]

    False [ ]

3. By relaxing when he could, Churchill felt he was ready for anything.

    True [ ]

    False [ ]

4. Balance is not needed for a fulfilling life.

    True [ ]

    False [ ]

5. Churchill had no physical limitations in his life.

    True [ ]

    False [ ]

PREP WORK Q & A

1. Why did Churchill rest when he could?

_____

_____

_____

_____

_____

2. Why is balance so important?

_____

_____

_____

_____

_____

3. Why did Churchill evaluate his performance at the end of each day?

_____

_____

_____

_____

_____

CHECKLIST

___Understand why we must have balance.

___Decide if you've been giving yourself enough down time.

___Come up with a plan to bring more balance in your life.

___Evaluate each day and see if you could find more balance.

FUN BREAK 2 OF 3

Wow your making great progress, keep it up. This crossword puzzle is a little harder than your last fun break. Do your best to solve it without using the answer sheet on the next page. Once you're done let's get back to learning.

<u>**Across**</u>: →
1. A distraction from an unpleasant reality
4. an idea in opposition to another idea
6. To endure or face without fear
10. A firm trust or belief in something
13. The state or situation of being alone
14. A person known to be self centered
15. The name of an L.A. baseball team

<u>**Down**</u>: ↓
2. An experienced or trusted adviser
3. Hostile behavior or opposition
5. The author of this book
7. A famous French Emperors first name
8. Complete absence of sound
9. Quick to detect or respond to changes
11. To try to acquire or develop
12. A feeling of uncertainty

FUN BREAK 2 OF 3 ANSWER SHEET

Across: →
1. A distraction from an unpleasant reality
4. an idea in opposition to another idea
6. To endure or face without fear
10. A firm trust or belief in something
13. The state or situation of being alone
14. A person known to be self centered
15. The name of an L.A. baseball team

Down: ↓
2. An experienced or trusted adviser
3. Hostile behavior or opposition
5. The author of this book
7. A famous French Emperors first name
8. Complete absence of sound
9. Quick to detect or respond to changes
11. To try to acquire or develop
12. A feeling of uncertainty

CHAPTER 24: SAY NO

Fabius was given orders to take over the Roman forces to stop Hannibal the conqueror. However, he did not send the legions in to immediately expel the warlord and send him back to Africa. Instead, he waited. To many this looked like weakness. In the eyes of many Roman critics, he did not act because he could not act and knew that Hannibal would overtake him. This was not the truth of it, however. It was part of his strategy.

Fabius knew that Hannibal was far away from home. He was losing men as they traveled and he could not easily replace these men. The elements would be their downfall. All Rome had to do was wait until they were weakened. The Roman people did not buy into this, however. They found this strategy insulting. They saw themselves as the strongest army in the world and thought it dishonorable, cowardly, weak, and a waste of time to wait. They urged action. So, while Fabius was attending a religious ceremony, the people pressured one of his commanders to attack. Minucius caved in to their pressure and attacked. He fell right into a trap. His men were being overwhelmed and Fabius had to enter the fray to help them escape.

Even though it was a near disaster, Minucius was *praised* for the failure. It was argued that *at least he tried*. Action, to many Romans, was respectable even if it ended in failure. Inaction could not be justified. Fabius returned to a defensive strategy until his term was served and finished. His successors would try a more aggressive strategy, only to fail miserably - losing half the army at the Battle of Cannae. They finally saw the benefit of Fabius, the great delayer.

There are times in life when it is beneficial to act often and act aggressively. In MLB scouting, players from around the globe will swing wildly to knock home runs out of the park. This ends up backfiring in the majors where better pitches take advantage of their wild swings. They have to train themselves to not swing and wait for the perfect pitch the same way Fabius wanted to wait for the perfect moment to engage Hannibal. Remember, traffic lights wouldn't work if they were always green. There's a moment to go. There's a moment to stop. As Mr. Roger's taught us, there's a moment to *slow down*. It's okay to pick your shots and get the most out of your actions.

KNOWLEDGE RETENTION TEST

1. Fabius had no strategy when asked to defeat Hannibal.

    True [ ]

    False [ ]

2. The Roman people asked someone else to go after Hannibal.

    True [ ]

    False [ ]

3. You should never act aggressively.

    True [ ]

    False [ ]

4. MLB players are encouraged to swing at every pitch.

    True [ ]

    False [ ]

5. It's important to pick your shots.

    True [ ]

    False [ ]

PREP WORK Q & A

1. Why did the Romans not like Fabius' strategy?

_____

_____

_____

_____

_____

2. How did Fabius' strategy end up being right in the end?

_____

_____

_____

_____

_____

3. Why should baseball players not swing at every pitch?

_____

_____

_____

_____

_____

CHECKLIST

___Understand how pacing yourself can be beneficial.

___Learn when it's important to wait.

___Develop patience.

___See how waiting can often be much more helpful in the end.

CHAPTER 25: TAKE A WALK

Soren Kierkegaard was an odd fellow. He would wake in the morning and write at a standing desk until he felt the need to take a walk. Then he would walk the city streets of Copenhagen in weird zig zags and sporadic motions. He never walked in a straight line. He likes to stick to the corners of streets, in the shade. Eventually he would think of an idea or get tired. He would return home and write for the rest of the evening. To most, it must seem like he was a nervous fellow; indeed, he was! Walking was how he worked out his anxiety so he could return to his writing with more clarity. He once wrote his bedridden sister about the benefits of walking. He urged her to keep her desire to walk. He noted that he walked himself into wellness every day and that there existed no thought so dark that you could not walk off. He is not alone in his praise of walking. Nietzsche, Tesla, Hemingway, Darwin, and Steve Jobs are some of many successful thinkers who took walks every day, sometimes multiple times per day.

Now, this might seem like another contradiction. We're supposed to be learning about stillness and walking is clearly motion! But it's a deliberate and repetitive motion. It's ritualized. A ritualized motion helps reign in the chaos of the mind and tame it towards peace and creativity. When you go on a walk you should be aware and open. You should be receptive to the world and take notice of the sights and be reflective about where your mind goes. Put your phone away. You shouldn't be transfixed on any one thing and your phone will take you away from your walk. Focus is not obsession. Breathe in and then out deliberately. Let your problems wash away as you try to imagine who or what might have walked in the very same spot centuries before. You might be walking in the same spot as a Tyrannosaurus! Walk away from whatever is bothering you.

You might arrive home to find that you haven't worked out your problems. Try walking in the other direction. Walk some more. If you're stressed about an assignment, do a portion of it and then take another walk. Walk until you've walked away from your anxiety and then walk a bit more. Build it into your routine.

KNOWLEDGE RETENTION TEST

1. Soren Kierkegaard felt walking was extremely beneficial.

   True [ ]

   False [ ]

2. Many great thinkers avoided taking walks.

   True [ ]

   False [ ]

3. Walking can help people reflect.

   True [ ]

   False [ ]

4. You should use your phone when taking a walk.

   True [ ]

   False [ ]

5. Walking can help with anxiety.

   True [ ]

   False [ ]

PREP WORK Q & A

1. How can walking help?

   _____

   _____

   _____

   _____

   _____

2. What should one focus on when walking?

   _____

   _____

   _____

   _____

   _____

3. What should you do if you walk and still haven't worked out your problems?

   _____

   _____

   _____

   _____

   _____

CHECKLIST

___Think about why walking is important.

___Work out a time you could walk regularly.

___Put your phone away while on a walk.

___Relax and allow your thoughts to roam while walking.

CHAPTER 26: BUILD A ROUTINE

Fred Rogers would wake every morning at the break of dawn and start to pray and think. Then, he would spend an hour swimming at the local fitness club. He would always weigh himself when he stepped out of the pool and made sure he weighed the same thing every time; he thought this an important element of health. Emerging from that pool at the end of his morning routine was like his own personal baptism that he got to experience every day. He would then go perform his show, the one we discussed with the yellow stop light reminding everyone to slow down. In that show, he would follow the same routine of taking off his shoes for more comfortable slippers. After the show, his routine would continue with a nap, dinner, time with family, and an early bed time to start the ritual again the next day. This might sound boring to some but for many it is absolutely essential for a fulfilling life.

Rogers isn't alone. Sports is filled with stars like Russel Westbrook who follow a routine before each game. His includes a peanut butter and jelly sandwich cut on an angle. These are successful people, often millionaires, who are deciding to cage themselves in a routine. Why? Isn't routine the opposite of freedom?

Most successful people know that complete freedom is Hell on Earth. The world is chaotic enough on its own and you do yourself no favors by adding to its hectic nature. Routine habits provide safeguards against the unpredictability of life and allow you to accomplish great things. Eisenhower defined freedom as the opportunity to discipline yourself through your own will. The daily cadence of a well-thought and purposefully acted ritual becomes like a religious experience that can cleanse the mind and body, much like the walks in the previous chapter. Routines are often time-based. Mr. Rogers and Jack Dorsey (founder of Twitter) get up at 5 AM. Jocko Willink, NAVY Seal, gets up at 4:30 AM and posts a picture of his watch as proof. Routines can also be focused on orderliness, such as cleaning your room when you wake up. It's not about magic or some superstition. You're not trying to summon anything with these rituals beyond the sense of order in your own mind which will help you stabilize yourself. If you are to master your mind you must master your day-to-day actions and a routine is a great place to start.

KNOWLEDGE RETENTION TEST

1. Fred Rogers had a daily routine that he stuck to.

   True [ ]

   False [ ]

2. A routine does not help with stillness.

   True [ ]

   False [ ]

3. Many successful people have routines.

   True [ ]

   False [ ]

4. A good routine can be like a religious experience for some.

   True [ ]

   False [ ]

5. A routine can help calm the mind.

   True [ ]

   False [ ]

PREP WORK Q & A

1. Why can a routine help your mind?

    _____

    _____

    _____

    _____

    _____

2. What does a routine give you?

    _____

    _____

    _____

    _____

    _____

3. Describe a famous person's routine.

    _____

    _____

    _____

    _____

    _____

CHECKLIST

___Think about your day.

___Decide if you already have some sort of routine.

___Evaluate if you could improve your routine or create one.

___Keep working on your routine to find one that works for you.

CHAPTER 27: GET RID OF YOUR STUFF

Epictetus was born a slave but came to earn his freedom. Soon enough, he himself was enjoying the good life and the fruits of his labor with many belongings and a nice home. One night, he rose to find that someone had stolen his favorite lamp! It was one of his most prized belongings. He felt violated and started to feel angry but then he stopped himself and remembered that a man can only lose what he has. He decided to buy a less expensive lamp the next day and he kept it for the rest of his life. Ironically, one of Epictetus' fans bought the lamp for a near-fortune upon his death.

A slave owner is really owned by his slaves. The man in a giant home is owned by it and not the other way around. These are the ideas Seneca taught. The items we have are meant only for their usefulness. We are not meant to be used by them. When we define ourselves by our fortunes and the items we have, we become slaves to them.

Philosophers don't always agree but limiting your material possessions is a common teaching in both Eastern and Western philosophy. From Buddhist Monks to Jesus, having too many things is not seen as a virtue. So how do you start?

Grab a trash bag and start walking around your home. You'll need two bags, actually. One is for actual trash and the other is for things you're going to give away. Give away anything that you don't use. It might be useful for someone else. Remember that the best clothes are the ones that allow for comfort and utility. The best car is the one that is reliable and farthest from your mind, not the one that will draw the most attention. Get the cheaper house with fewer bedrooms, etc. What's the point of having extra, empty rooms if you have to work more just to pay it off and never share it with anyone? From the micro and macro, you can limit your material possessions to better free your mind and field of vision. Give away all that tech that you never use that didn't bring you the joy that you thought it would. Take back your life.

KNOWLEDGE RETENTION TEST

1. We are slaves to our things.

    True [ ]

    False [ ]

2. Having lots of expensive things is important.

    True [ ]

    False [ ]

3. Expensive items show others how hard you've worked.

    True [ ]

    False [ ]

4. The best car is dependable.

    True [ ]

    False [ ]

5. Limiting your possessions can help you see clearer.

    True [ ]

    False [ ]

PREP WORK Q & A

1. How is a slave owner really owned by his slaves?

_____

_____

_____

_____

_____

2. How does limiting your possessions free you?

_____

_____

_____

_____

_____

3. Describe how you can clear out your things.

_____

_____

_____

_____

_____

CHECKLIST

___Look around your home.

___Get two bags, one for trash and one for donating.

___Go through everything you own and get rid of anything you don't need.

___Downsize wherever possible.

CHAPTER 28: SEEK SOLITUDE

Leonardo da Vinci wrote stories in his notebooks to get his thoughts out. In one of these fables, a solitary rock sat among beautiful flowers and herbs. Down below was the road where the other rocks were and he desired to be among their number. So, he rolled down the bottom of the hill to be with his fellow rocks. It wasn't everything he had hoped it would be.

The stone was walked over, covered in horse feces, chipped away, and all manner of troubling pains. What's worse is that the rock would sometimes get glimpses of the home he had left behind. Da Vinci argued that this is what happens to people when they move to big cities which were filled with sinful people.

Of course, that wasn't practical advice for Leonardo to follow. He lived most of his life in busy cities, where the patrons were. The same is true for us. The necessities of life often require us to live in busy environments. That's why carving out time and space for solitude is essential; we won't get it otherwise. While working on *The Last Supper,* da Vinci would seek out solitude to go over his thoughts and clear his head for the creative challenge ahead of him.

Relationships are vital. However, it's difficult to understand yourself and what you can bring to other people if you are never alone. If you're constantly roaming from one party to the next or if your home is filled with people - working through your thoughts can be a near-impossible task. You can't master stillness if you don't have silence and you can't have silence without a healthy, daily dose of solitude. Why don't you have solitude? Because you don't take the time to schedule solitude into your day. Each of us needs to take this time to cultivate in solitude. Thomas Merton showed that silent solitude was an active experience if you approach it with discipline and vigilance. If you absorb your solitude and truly live that experience, you will benefit from it. Merton realized that after spending so much time in solitude, that it became a part of him. Any time he felt overwhelmed he could bring himself into that state of solitude. So, make sure you take time to schedule your solitude.

KNOWLEDGE RETENTION TEST

1. Leonardo DaVinci sometimes wrote stories to get his thoughts out.

   True [ ]

   False [ ]

2. We don't need to seek out solitude in our busy lives.

   True [ ]

   False [ ]

3. Scheduling time to be alone is important for each of us.

   True [ ]

   False [ ]

4. DaVinci believed that cities were filled with sinful people.

   True [ ]

   False [ ]

5. It's impossible to find solitude in cities.

   True [ ]

   False [ ]

PREP WORK Q & A

1. Why is it hard to find stillness in a city?

_____

_____

_____

_____

_____

2. Why is it important to balance relationships and alone time?

_____

_____

_____

_____

_____

3. What should you do to make sure you get solitude each day?

_____

_____

_____

_____

_____

CHECKLIST

___Take a look at your schedule.

___Ensure you have time to be alone.

___If you don't, find the time.

___Make time to be alone each day.

CHAPTER 29: BE A HUMAN BEING

Horses die of work. It's important to remember to strike a balance in everything. Any virtue is a vice taken when taken to an extreme. Prince Albert exemplified many of the positive qualities of discipline and conservatism associated with the Victorian era. He took up many of Queen Victoria's burdens and found ways to streamline processes. Together, they were proud work horses. They took on every responsibility available and gained the corresponding influence. Prince Albert would sometimes throw up from the pressure and then continue working.

There was great benefit in understanding geopolitics and the decision to stay out of the American Civil War. But Albert knew no moderation. He spent years of his life planning a carnival. He never said no to an opportunity and the stress was overbearing. He once wrote his mother stating that he was more dead than alive. Victoria was constantly pregnant. It's like the two never stopped working.

While Britain benefited from all the work, it eventually killed Albert. He died of Crohn's disease which was worsened by his stress. Do you want to live like Albert, constantly pushing through pain and 'toughing it out'? It's good to be a soldier sometimes but we also must remember that soldiers die. High-level athletes overuse their bodies until they don't work anymore. You must remember that you are trying to maximize your benefit through your life, which will not happen if you max yourself out during the short term. Athletes who pace themselves and take regular rest tend to have longer, more successful careers than those who always go at 100% in training. Remember the lie that was hung by the Nazis at Auschwitz: Work will set you free.

People running on empty don't work well and If you're in a hurry, you will make more mistakes. You might try to be useful but you are no use to anyone when you are in a panic. Calm down. Things will take care of themselves. Just slow down, think them out, and act accordingly. Take breaks when you need them and you will definitely need them. Protect your body above all, as you only get one. There are times when you can push yourself, just make sure it's not all the time. Make sure you get some rest.

KNOWLEDGE RETENTION TEST

1. Horses will work until they die.

    True [ ]

    False [ ]

2. Prince Albert loved working under stress.

    True [ ]

    False [ ]

3. High level athlete's bodies give out sooner.

    True [ ]

    False [ ]

4. It's good to push yourself harder.

    True [ ]

    False [ ]

5. Panic helps people think clearer.

    True [ ]

    False [ ]

PREP WORK Q & A

1. What effects did stress have on Prince Albert?

_____

_____

_____

_____

_____

2. How can stress affect the body?

_____

_____

_____

_____

_____

3. How often should a person rest?

_____

_____

_____

_____

_____

CHECKLIST

___Think about your work life.

___Consider if your home life is stressful also.

___Decide if you're getting enough rest.

___Don't push yourself too hard for too long.

CHAPTER 30: GO TO SLEEP

Dov Charney founded American Apparel and kept an open-door policy even when it evolved into an international corporation making almost a billion dollars per year. Any employee at any level of the company could get in touch with Dov about anything to do with the company. It made Charney constantly involved with his growing company and had benefits early on, taking advantage of opportunities and fixing problems as they arose. However, this policy would soon take its toll.

Think about it. When the company grew to 250 stores, there would always be someone who had an issue. Charney was barely sleeping. By the end, he wasn't sleeping at all. The more successful his company was the less sleep he was able to get because he never unplugged from the business. It's one of the primary reasons the company went under. Charney lost the ability to function adequately enough to make good decisions and spent too much time on things that didn't matter more than his health. At one point Charney moved into a distribution warehouse with nothing but a bed and shower. While this might seem like a heroic act of dedication, the blind loyalty to the mission actually kept him from functioning. Charney descended into madness in front of his employees and American Apparel was doomed.

A 2017 study showed that a lack of sleep leads the mind to repeatedly think negatively. Your mind will actually abuse itself if you don't sleep. If you're a hard-working engineer chugging 5 cans of Monster Energy, do you really think you have a chance at stillness? Will the work really get done correctly? You might hit your due date but with a product at half its quality. The truth is, if you want to be your best possible self, you have to sleep.

KNOWLEDGE RETENTION TEST

1. The owner of American Apparel was never available to his employees.

    True [ ]

    False [ ]

2. American Apparel went under because the owner never got to rest.

    True [ ]

    False [ ]

3. Sleep is necessary for your physical health.

    True [ ]

    False [ ]

4. Performance suffers when a person is too tired.

    True [ ]

    False [ ]

5. Drinking lots of caffeine reverses the effects of not sleeping.

    True [ ]

    False [ ]

124

PREP WORK Q & A

1. Why did American Apparel go under?

_____

_____

_____

_____

_____

2. Why is sleep important?

_____

_____

_____

_____

_____

3. How can being too involved be a downfall?

_____

_____

_____

_____

_____

CHECKLIST

___Pay attention to how much sleep you regularly get.

___Cut out substances that can affect your sleep.

___Learn how much rest your body requires.

___Make sure you get it.

CHAPTER 31: FIND A HOBBY

We've discussed one prime minister, Churchill, but one before his generation presents some unique insight. William Gladstone had a unique hobby. He liked to venture into the woods on his property and chop down giant trees with nothing but his hands and an axe. He spent two days in a row in 1876 chopping away at a girthy elm tree. This was just one of a thousand times he ventured into the woods to chop away with his axe. He would bring his family on occasion and make a bonding moment out of it. The process was so focus-consuming that he couldn't think of anything else while he was out there chopping away.

Churchill's father actually criticized Gladstone as being destructive. He was one of many who looked down on chopping trees. But Gladstone was very particular about the trees he chopped down and argued that he simply removed the stuffy, old trees to make way for the healthy trees - the same thing he does in politics (his joke was well received).

Gladstone was an effective leader but he was stressed like all men in positions of power. His hobby helped him alleviate much of this stress and it's unlikely that he could have coped without such an activity. The great swordsman Musashi took up painting and said each art enhanced the other. Basketball champion Chris Bosh knows how to code in computer languages. Einstein had a violin. Leisure activities are defined by the active part. They help reset and focus the mind. It's not about being lazy or doing nothing. It's about deliberately doing something challenging that you are interested in that has nothing to do with mere survival. It's not something that you do for pay or to impress anyone. It's something you do to improve yourself because you genuinely want to get better at the activity.

There's nothing to feel guilty about when doing leisurely activities. Your mental health and your ability to be still depends on it. It will pay dividends, even though it doesn't pay in immediate monetary gains. Some things are more important. Just make sure that your hobby is not an escape.

KNOWLEDGE RETENTION TEST

1. Prime Minister William Gladstone cut down trees with his bare hands and an axe.

   True [ ]

   False [ ]

2. Gladstone's hobby of cutting down trees helped him cope with stress.

   True [ ]

   False [ ]

3. Not everyone needs a hobby.

   True [ ]

   False [ ]

4. Hobbies should make you money.

   True [ ]

   False [ ]

5. It's only a hobby if you're really good at it.

   True [ ]

   False [ ]

PREP WORK Q & A

1. Why did Gladstone cut down trees?

   _____

   _____

   _____

   _____

   _____

2. How can a hobby help with stress?

   _____

   _____

   _____

   _____

3. Is it important what kind of a hobby a person has?

   _____

   _____

   _____

   _____

CHECKLIST

___Think about things you do outside of work.

___Consider what your hobbies are.

___If you don't have one, make a list of things that interest you.

___Begin trying out hobbies.

FUN BREAK 3 OF 3

You've made it to the final fun break. This one will really test your skill. The words below are all from this book and can be hidden across, down, diagonal and backwards. Enjoy the final fun break then let's get back to learning. (Answer sheet on next page)

```
Y  D  G  M  L  V  J  I  C  T  K  N  T  W  V  I  R  T  U  E  D  R  N
Z  O  X  E  N  O  U  G  H  U  W  E  E  X  X  Q  Y  T  P  M  E  L  Y
J  U  R  Z  C  H  E  G  K  I  L  N  N  E  M  U  Y  B  P  K  B  Q  B
X  B  S  E  C  L  H  X  H  D  R  T  W  Z  B  E  A  U  T  Y  K  X  B
N  T  E  C  I  M  U  I  L  E  Z  K  I  D  O  H  W  W  T  E  J  C  O
S  D  Y  N  F  S  O  P  T  S  K  M  B  V  O  J  O  R  P  X  R  X  H
U  K  O  E  B  I  S  E  J  I  U  D  M  O  A  G  V  W  B  T  O  K  D
D  I  J  L  V  C  A  O  A  R  B  S  I  W  U  T  O  S  F  E  T  E  B
Z  O  A  I  P  I  W  G  U  E  K  V  N  G  Y  T  E  L  K  N  N  E  R
L  T  M  S  M  O  Q  E  E  L  K  J  D  L  D  M  W  A  I  D  E  S  A
R  B  D  A  K  T  S  G  V  N  L  X  V  L  I  N  C  B  M  A  M  C  V
H  H  A  D  I  S  G  O  J  J  D  W  I  S  D  O  M  N  Y  B  T  G  E
O  T  V  R  K  N  Q  R  T  Y  C  A  G  V  E  L  Z  S  E  A  O  H  H
Z  M  I  L  R  N  A  P  P  B  C  E  E  X  C  N  L  Z  K  N  Q  R  V
L  R  D  N  W  L  E  A  R  S  I  D  L  P  I  I  N  P  U  T  R  V  C
G  D  D  G  J  M  P  Z  P  S  E  W  P  E  E  L  S  V  P  F  Z  M  T
```

Find the following words in the puzzle.
Words are hidden ↑ ↓ → ← and ↘ .

AGENDA	EGO	JOY	SOUL
BEAUTY	EMPTY	KENZO	STOICISM
BRAVE	ENOUGH	KEY	VIRTUE
CULTIVATE	EXTEND	MENTOR	WISDOM
DAVID	GOLIATH	MIND	
DESIRE	HOBBY	SEEK	
DOMAIN	INPUT	SILENCE	
DOUBT	ISRAEL	SLEEP	

FUN BREAK 3 OF 3 ANSWER SHEET

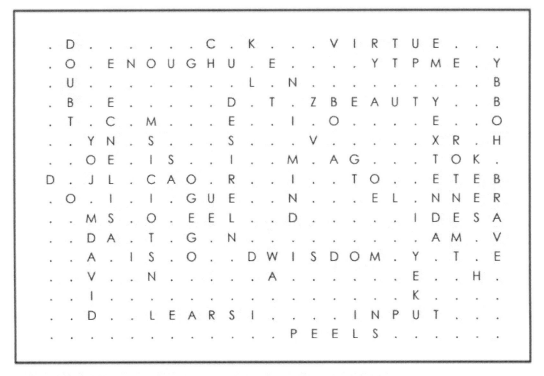

Word directions and start points are formatted: (Direction, X, Y)

AGENDA (SE,7,8)
BEAUTY (E,15,4)
BRAVE (S,23,8)
CULTIVATE (SE,9,1)
DAVID (S,3,11)
DESIRE (S,10,4)
DOMAIN (SE,1,8)
DOUBT (S,2,1)

EGO (S,8,10)
EMPTY (W,21,2)
ENOUGH (E,4,2)
EXTEND (S,20,5)
GOLIATH (SE,16,7)
HOBBY (N,23,6)
INPUT (E,16,15)
ISRAEL (W,11,15)

JOY (N,3,8)
KENZO (SE,11,1)
KEY (N,19,14)
MENTOR (N,21,11)
MIND (S,13,7)
SEEK (N,22,10)
SILENCE (N,4,10)
SLEEP (W,17,16)

SOUL (SE,7,7)
STOICISM (N,6,12)
VIRTUE (E,15,1)
WISDOM (E,12,12)

CHAPTER 32: BEWARE ESCAPISM

John Fante was a successful Hollywood screenwriter but the town broke his heart when his novel was a flop. He needed an escape but he was too invested in his career and too married to just leave town. He took to playing pinball and drinking for hours on end. This is different than seeking a leisurely activity. This is not restorative. It's a form of escape.

It's the intention that matters. Travel can be a rewarding experience but when you're traveling just 'to get away', it reduces the activity to a form of escape. Escape is the 500 movies Nixon watched during his darkest days. It's Tiger Woods drug addiction. Escapism gives us no real benefits aside from a temporary rush and a superficial relief from our daily stress. It doesn't have the restorative benefit of a leisurely activity. You're trying to defer your life to a later moment. You're putting off your stillness for another day. However, that bill always comes and it will arrive with interest the more you put it off.

Emerson pointed out that the sights that travelers like to visit are not built by travelers. They were built by people fixed to a spot with a job to get something done. There's no amount of answers you can find by traveling to some far-off land. It's not going to solve your problems. Being still sometimes means remaining still, where you are. Whether you're trying to escape to the bottom of a bottle or across the globe, you will not find answers there. You must do the work of stillness where that work is. You must meet it there. You have to stay still for a long while and find out what you're trying to escape from and meet it with all that you are, or you will keep paying taxes on that 'bill' for the rest of your life. **Build a life that you don't want to escape from.**

KNOWLEDGE RETENTION TEST

1. John Emerson's novel was a success.

    True [ ]

    False [ ]

2. Some hobbies can be bad.

    True [ ]

    False [ ]

3. Using a hobby to avoid problems is called escapism.

    True [ ]

    False [ ]

4. Escapism is always good.

    True [ ]

    False [ ]

5. We should all try to build a life we don't want to escape from.

    True [ ]

    False [ ]

PREP WORK Q & A

1. What is escapism?

_____

_____

_____

_____

_____

2. How is escapism different from resting?

_____

_____

_____

_____

_____

3. Describe a situation where someone is using escapism.

_____

_____

_____

_____

_____

CHECKLIST

____Take another look at your hobbies.

____Determine if they are good for you.

____Consider if they might be how you escape.

____If they are, find a new hobby.

CHAPTER 33: ACT BRAVELY

Clamence is the narrator in the novel *The Fall.* He's walking the streets of Amsterdam when he thinks he hears a woman make a noise and fall into the water. He isn't exactly sure what it is he hears and decides to ignore the sound, especially because he is having a great night with his mistress. He continues on with his life as always has, a successful lawyer.

However, something feels different. Something is off. He has a successful day in court but then he feels he is being mocked. He isn't sure by who or where. He just has the feeling he is being shamed. Later that day he approaches a motorist who is stalled in the road and is assaulted. While these are not connected, he feels a general weakening in his perception of himself and the life he has built. Slowly, he realizes that he had the chance to save someone from suicide but did not take it. His perception of himself as a good person shatters and he unwinds. The sound of that woman haunts him for the rest of his days as he walks the street hoping for the chance to save someone else, a chance that never comes.

This isn't a true story but the lesson rings true. Your thoughts and work might be very admiral but they are nothing if you do not act in accordance with your values. The health of your spirit depends on what you choose to do with your body. Anne Dufourmantelle was a French philosopher who died in 2017 at a beach, Pampelonne, while trying to rescue two children who were drowning. The two children survived but Anne could not be saved. She often wrote about risk in her philosophy, arguing that risk was inevitable and saw risk taking as an essential part of life and growth. She lived up to her values and ideals and died taking the risk to save those children. Would it have been better to survive, watch the children die, and go on as a coward? Hardly. Anne died living up to her ideals. If you know that something is the right thing to do, you should do it.

Stillness is not about escape. It's not about being separate from the world. It's about being connected to the world and bringing everything you are to bear upon its troubles. Being still allows you to bring more goodness into the world. Virtue is something that must be acted out which raises the quality of humanity. It's not some motionless quality of the human soul. Values must be cultivated and used for the betterment of the world you were lucky enough to be born into.

If you want to feel good you have to do good things for others. If you don't, you will realize it and you will have to live with your lack of action for the rest of your life. You will never be still if you do not act bravely.

KNOWLEDGE RETENTION TEST

1. The novel The Fall is about a man who falls off a bridge.

    True [ ]

    False [ ]

2. It doesn't matter how you act if your heart is in the right place.

    True [ ]

    False [ ]

3. Stillness is about being separate from others.

    True [ ]

    False [ ]

4. It's important to always be brave.

    True [ ]

    False [ ]

5. There is never a need to help others.

    True [ ]

    False [ ]

PREP WORK Q & A

1. What is the novel The Fall about?

    _____

    _____

    _____

    _____

    _____

2. What is bravery to you?

    _____

    _____

    _____

    _____

    _____

3. Why is it important to be brave?

    _____

    _____

    _____

    _____

    _____

CHECKLIST

___Reflect on your life.

___Consider if there have been times you've acted bravely.

___Recall any times you didn't.

___Compare both times and find out what was different.

CHAPTER 34: ON TO THE FINAL ACT

Antoninus Pius was dying and he knew it. He called his son Marcus Aurelius into the room to transfer over the empire to him. He then turned to his audience and said his final word, which meant 'imperturbability'. A few hundred years earlier, the Buddha similarly gathered his disciples for his final words. He knew that they were frightened that they would no longer have a teacher but he assured them that they would be their own teachers. He told them to seek their freedom with dignity. Epicurus, who lived and died in the years between Antoninus and the Buddha, also knew he was going to die and wrote a letter in which he emphasized clarity. He died a few hours after writing the letter, joining the other great thinkers who had already passed.

Seneca reminded us that death is just a return to the state we were in before we were born. This is true for all of us. Yet, we fight in insignificant squabbles as if they are important. As if we will live forever. Cicero put it right: philosophy is the study of learning how to die. While this book is about living well, it's really about dying with grace. We're all going to die in ultimate stillness and we should prepare for it. One day your mind, body, and soul will be united in a single state (even if that state is nothingness). The same is true of before your birth. Finding such a balance while still alive is a struggle and one worth going through. Death makes everything still and brings an end to everything, as we must also end this book.

ABOUT GROWTH HACK BOOKS

Here at Growth Hack Books our goal is to save you time by providing the best workbooks possible. We stand out from our competitors by not only including all of the pertinent facts from the subject book but also knowledge retention tests after each chapter, a Prep work Q & A section after each chapter that allows you to document the steps you will take to reach your goals, easy to follow summaries of each chapter including checklists and even puzzles and games to make learning more interesting.

As you can see, we go above and beyond to make your purchase a pleasant one. If you learned something beneficial from this book please leave a positive review so others can benefit as well. Lastly if you haven't yet make sure you purchase the subject book, Stillness is the Key, by visiting https://amzn.to/2IInGGx

Made in the USA
Columbia, SC
24 September 2022

67892157R00090